Safe Passage

A Memoir in Poetry and Prose

Anne Sherry

ASHBROOK
Publications

First Edition: Safe Passage

First Published in Great Britain in 2014 by:
ASHBROOK Publications
via annesherry@madasafish.com

ISBN 978-0-9927930-0-5

British Library Cataloguing Publication Data. A CIP record for this book can be obtained from the British Library.

Typeset in Times New Roman by *ASHBROOK* Publications

Cover design by Chris Maynard of Design Matters, photograph Shutterstock – ©Igor Sokolov (breeze)

Colophon by Tim Farrell based on an idea by Albert Grazeley

Printed and bound in Great Britain by CPI Group (UK), Croydon, CR0 4YY

For John

'Only in as much as my life, or anything in my life, corresponds to true things in other people's lives, is it of interest, and this depends on telling the deep truths: and the surface facts are just relieving frills, a few little restful thrills, a bit of colour in the bare garden.'

Elizabeth Smart

Acknowledgements

Thanks are due to the editors of the following journals in which some of the poems in this memoir have appeared: Magma, Pennine Platform, South, Weyfarers and various Norwich Writers' Open Poetry Competition Anthologies.

My thanks also to my family, friends and fellow writers for their support and encouragement, particularly Stephen Smith, the late Colin Archer, Roger Garfitt and the Madingley Masterclass, the members of the Winchester Poetry Workshop, Linda Ewles, Cynthia Jewell and Tim Farrell.

And above all, to Michael Knight, without whom so much would not have been possible.

Contents

Alone

Epilogue

Prologue

The Genoa charcoal hung above the fireplace in Farnborough. When I moved to Winchester I placed it opposite the sofa, slightly left of centre, on the cream-white wall. An original, bought in the early 90s from an art student, the charcoal is a large, line drawing on white vellum. Abstract yet very definite.

Four simple fishing boats, the largest angled to the right, two to the left and a smudged fourth in the distance. Like ducks flying out of formation. Or rowing boats adrift on a flat sea. Around them criss-crossed lines, in soft grey and sturdy black, represent ropes and waves. Bizarrely, behind the boats, there is a VTOL, a vertical take-off landing jet, with a globe-shaped aura above the folded wings and, below, vertical jet thrusts. It could be a Bell Boeing Osprey or a Harrier. I recognise both from living with an aircraft engineer. The jet is coming in to land, heading straight for the boats, skimming the rowlocks. I find the thought disturbing, as if a fish eagle were pouncing on unsuspecting kittiwakes. But I like the picture's ambivalence: air and sea, tradition and progress, noise and silence, calm and threat. Despite the fish eagle-fighter jet the picture works. It has a good aura.

Like a Rorschach ink blot, experience clearly led me to this interpretation. I'd been in Genoa on business, carrying out a Human Resources audit for United Distillers. The flight over the Alps and down to the coast was breathtaking, as was the landing. We circled long and low over the waves, eventually pitching on a bony finger of land. Years later, landing in a twelve-seat prop plane on a strip of grass in a Costa Rican jungle was significantly less petrifying. At least in Costa Rica there were trees to cushion any overrun; off Genoa, nothing but a watery grave.

After John's death I spent hours, days, weeks, sitting, looking, doing nothing. Silent, closed in with my grief. No TV, no music, no radio, no reading, I existed, eating when hungry, sleeping when tired. I existed; I didn't live. It was worse after the funeral. The phone stopped ringing, the flood of cards dried up. Others went on with their lives leaving me with mine, such as it was. Dregs and dashed hopes. I zoned out the noise next door – carpenters building a decked patio for my young neighbours – as

I'd done the week of the funeral with the other side. For six weeks I lived in a void.

In the seventh week I put on a CD, cried along with Elgar's Second Symphony. Then I read some Yeats. His Collected Works had been on the coffee table the day of the funeral; seven weeks later the Collection was still there. I re-read the words on the cover, words that had helped me through:

> There on the scaffolding reclines Michael Angelo
> With no more sound than the mice make
> His hand moves to and fro
> Like a long-legged fly upon the stream
> His mind moves upon silence.

I located the source, 'Long-legged Fly.'

For two more weeks, like Michael Angelo, my mind moved upon silence. Another two before I watched Master Chef the Professionals. Five months later I still couldn't (still can't) tolerate John Humphreys in the morning. The Genoa charcoal was at one with that silent world. Its starkness mirrored my own. Aesthetic, pared down, minimalist, essential – and comforting.

Why did I look more closely? Possibly, because I wanted to start sketching again. Something creative to do when my eyes were too tired to read. My drawing materials were in a box on the floor below the charcoal. Or was the charcoal calling me? One evening, I went up close and really looked at that jet fighter. Twenty years on I could see it was nothing like a jet fighter. Not even a British Airways airbus ferrying business passengers in from Gatwick.

That globe-shaped kerosene aura is a mandala of light streaming from a lighthouse. The body of the jet is a lighthouse, its wings the Ligurian coastline. The smudged vertical jet thrusts are reflected light. As seductive as a green flash.

I stand, on pause. For twenty years I've been living with a fish eagle-jet fighter instead of the Genoese coastline. Might there be other things that I've seen inaccurately? Nietzche's words come to mind, 'out of chaos came forth a dancing star.'

I decide to go back.

Together

Handles and Emotional Intelligence

1983. Travelling north from Valras-Plage in the Languedoc we stopped at Cahors. Our guide, Arthur Eperon, had given it unconditional approval. Here I learnt an important lesson. I clearly wasn't endowed with any emotional intelligence or much patience in those days. Happily I've since developed the first; less though, the second.

Despite Eperon, or possibly because of him, we have trouble finding a room. We park the Mondeo and plod the warp and weft of Cahors. *Complet* everywhere. Eventually in a tiny side street we spot a sign, the Lion D'Or, its gilt well tarnished. John opens the door. At the back another slams. A couple are arguing loudly, their Lot accents generously peppered with expletives. I pick up at least four *merdes*. Hmm, I think. However needs must.

'Allo! Allo!' I call out. The arguing stops, then resumes, slightly louder. A woman's voice, shrill, 'Boff! Qu'est-ce que t'en penses?' I try again, same reaction plus another exceptionally emphatic *merde!* Third attempt.

'Allo! Allo!' I call, ignoring John, who's backing into the street.

Crash! The sound of breaking glass as a red-faced Frenchman in a grubby vest –- no sign of Gallic sartorial elegance here – pops my personal space bubble.

'Bonjour Monsieur, avez-vous une chambre pour la nuit?' I smile. He looks at me, using every single atom of *non-foutisme* only a Frenchman can summon. Then he barks '*Non!*' with twice the force of De Gaulle rejecting UK entry into the Common Market.

'I could see that coming,' chortles John as we scurry off.

We do eventually find a hotel (fifth floor, no lift) and, later, a table at Mon Auberge. Both service and presentation disappoint although the food sings. *Escargots* and *soupe de poisson*; *confit de canard* and *bavette au vin*; *glace à la vanille* and John's perennial *tarte aux pommes*. In my family, for patently obvious reasons to me, the edge of pastry crust on a tart or pie has always been known as a 'handle.' That's what you hold it by, isn't it? Obviously therefore, a handle. What else would you call it? John had always found this hilarious.

The 'handle' at Mon Auberge is somewhat overcooked; in fact it is as black as coal. So much for Eperon's recommendation. Perhaps the chef was *en vacances.*

'Ze 'andle on zees tart ees veree black!' I say.

And here is John at his lovable best: that ready sense of humour, the enormous, fat laugh, always appreciating a joke. Tonight all three are enhanced by a bottle of full-bodied black Cahors wine. The waiter is not amused. Madame la Patronne's face morphs into a preserved fig. She must have been related to Monsieur *Non*! We, on the other hand, roar like the runaway train that went over the hill; we blow.

Thirty years on as I type I start to giggle. Then I'm laughing out loud, clutching my sides, wiping away *je m'en fous* tears. I guffaw myself out of grief and back to Cahors.

Arthur Eperon, *Traveller's France*, 1979, Pan Books.

The Sofa

I feel warm. Something soft and smooth is covering me. I'm surrounded by cushions. There's a swishing in my ears. I swallow twice but the swishing stays. My head echoes and buzzes, a bee in my brain. My eyes ache. I've been away; now I'm back. Safe.

The room is dark, in shadow, the curtains drawn shut. The room is fragrant – with beeswax, fir-cones, roasting chestnuts, cigar smoke. A special place.

I uncurl, stretch out my right leg, test space, locate a padded wooden block. The patchwork cover slips. As I catch it, I peer at the surface I'm lying on. The material is dark and patterned with leaves, nasturtiums, spots and petals. It's soft but not uniformly so. Tiny folds of knobbly dralon ridge under my stroking fingers. The design is comforting, bright splashes on brown. Autumn colours.

I feel around. The velvet surface curves towards the floor. Stocky wooden legs planted under a full skirt. I squint in the dappled light. Family history lives in this perfumed place. Precious times long gone, half forgotten.

I've been crying; I still am. The pillow is wet. I recognise both tears and sofa in the same instant.

Our wonderful sofa. A dumpy monstrosity of a thing. Chunky arms beneath swathed upholstery. A curved back and a matching curved seat. Uncomfortable to sit on, designed for well-behaved children who sit up straight on high days and holidays. The sofa lives in our front room. How I love this sofa. It is dependable.

We are never allowed in the front room on our own. Normally we bunch up together in the living room of our Mother Hubbard house. But sometimes I steal an event preview. I think Nanny knows but she never tells.

I quietly open the door and stand very still, breathing in the atmosphere. And then, heart thundering, I slip inside. I sit on the sofa. Like a dormouse. I don't kick the skirt the way we do at Christmas. I just sit in that bone china room, silent except for the slow, cosy ticking of the clock and an occasional, distant car.

Never ever a speck of dust. A few ornaments on the mantelpiece, a sheep stuck to a tree trunk and a green Silvana vase. The mottled beige fireplace has a broken tile. Magnolia walls. A neutral frame for the solid sofa.

Here I can hear myself think. Far away from the daily scramble for airtime, affection and space. I can remember last Christmas, look forward to the next.

Adult voices whisper nearby, hesitant. My parents creep into the room. Mum puts her hand on my forehead. My father pulls the cover up.

'How are you feeling, love?'

'Sicky. I've got a headache.'

'I expect you have. It'll go off. You knocked yourself out on the wall.'

'How?'

'You were swinging to and fro on the back legs of the chair.' He doesn't say 'and I told you not to.' An unusual event; my father always knows best.

'We thought you'd like *this* until you feel better.'

This is pure magic. A flat, round painted tin, about six by three inches, gold and red with a wonderful picture of the young Queen and the Duke of Edinburgh on the lid. Brightly coloured, it smells of shortbread. Everyone covets the tin but no-one is allowed to have it. Equality is the name of the game in our family. Equality means being treated according to the lowest common denominator. And the lowest common denominator is never me.

'For keeps or just for a while?'

'For keeps,' Mum says. My father sniffs. 'Just don't swing on that chair again. You frightened us half to death.'

My sister, brothers, Nanny and the cat come in to see me. No-one says anything about not being able to balance, or misbehaving again, or provoking Dad. I am allowed to lie quietly on the sofa with *my* Coronation tin for the rest of the day.

Only afterwards do I have the heady thought that sometimes disobedience does pay off.

Family

Uncle's three-up, three-down
in a terracotta terrace, toy rooms,
lav in the yard by the coal-hole –
a plant would cheer things up –
OMO-bright tea, acres of cake,
talk as banal as blancmange.

The Minx climbs Portsdown Hill,
chugs through the Chalk Cut,
gathers strength and runs for home
as baby snuffles, two scrunch
into soft, sibling sleep; me,
I look back.

Decked with colour and light –
a glorious wide-open atlas –
Portsmouth unfurls to France
reaches out beyond Europe
stretches as far as forever;
I look back, dream forward.

> At Dad's wake I mention poetry.
> 'You were always like that –
> bookish, curious.' 'Preferred
> books to people, often still do.'
> 'Wicked, cous. *Now* I see why.'
> Carol grins, pours us more Pinot.

Swiss Army Knife

1986, Western Europe. Off again, in love with the open road, travel spoiling us for the regular life, 'moving from country to country, in blithe ignorance ... granted the safe passage' of idiots. Which is pretty much the way most of my subsequent life has turned out. I gently feel my way forward, one step at a time.

Belgium, hanging petrified in the cable car above Namur. 'Maybe we should call this town manure?' John suggested. Bouvignes sur Meuse, with the ruins of Crèvecoeur (heartbreak) Castle, Saint Hubert and an exhilarating round-town cycle race. 'Allez! Allez!' John bellowed, reliving his cycling days. Vianden, 'jewel of Luxembourg,' according to Victor Hugo. Selestat, in France, telegraph poles growing out of the house roofs. Down the Rhine into Germany: Meersburg on Lake Constance, where a school friend had taught; Mainau, the flower island, a big, fat oompah band playing in the square. Round the lake, through Austria into Switzerland.

We drove south from Lucerne, on and off the autobahn – tunnel after gallery after gallery after tunnel, a bucking bronco of a road that galloped south towards the Mediterranean. One tunnel was 9250 metres long; the mountains like scenes from Romantic poems. Tiredness evaporated as adrenalin kicked in. Villages, castles, monuments perched on hillsides, hair-brained hairpins, a dream drive. Past Altdorf, home-town of William Tell, then even sheerer drops, the car sandwiched between walls of rock. We lunched on a platform over a river, close to one of the motorway galleries, followed by a white-knuckle ride over the St Gotthard pass. At Andermatt, motorbikes everywhere, white-capped drivers in sporty Mercedes, flying up and down the passes while the tourists pottered. *Avoid queues, use the stopping places* pleaded the signs.

Into Swiss Ticino, along roads that sliced through mountains, skirted sheer drops, threatened falling rocks. Biasca 'c'est très simple ici, vous voyez,' to Locarno, a lovely road along the lake, views of tiny harbours, castles on islands, Italian signs. Petrol at Gazzanats, coffees at Casale Monferrato, loud voices, the air bright with Italian laughter.

And so Switzerland – and time – whizzed by.

June 2009. John died in April. Being seventeen years older – although he never seemed, or acted, as if he were – it was always on the cards that John would go before me. But, like this? No, never like this.

Now I'm travelling alone, by train – Zurich, Lucerne, Locarno, Lugano – at the suggestion of Greta, a German friend. 'Switzerland will do you good. They speak English and everything works. No stress. Just time and space. Just for you.'

Some days I think she's right, I do feel better. Other days I could thump that Teutonic practicality which normally I value so much. I'm still in deep grief. For years I've been keeping a personal journal. Like me, it's a mess of scribbled pages, filed randomly. In places, the writing's almost illegible.

21st: Dined with George and Jacqueline, a lecturer in criminology from Paris – they travel with a 50-litre suitcase. She wishes me sunshine and renewed well-being. I walk out of the dining room in tears.

23rd: The train south from Lucerne – miraculous – a child's drawing of a mountain landscape – roads, waterfalls, snow on mountain tops, bridges, tunnels, covered roadways, villages in valleys, pointy Gothic arches. Wonderful! The landscape of my youth; the landscape of happy times with John. Perhaps I could stay, live in that past?

24th: Missing John, missing worrying about John. Missing, missing, missing. Everything meaningless alone. Can't stop crying – five minutes to mop up then I start again. A bad, bad day. Grieving in Lugano. No better than in Winchester.

25th: Another awful day – one of the worst. Don't know what to do with myself. Can't stop crying. Tummy churning, nausea. Lonely, look like pooh. Whimpering 'I want my old life back.' Which life? When? Fragments of memory taunt me, happy times. Shit! Everything's shit!

27th: Drink in bar with Brummie couple. 'You must feel a great sense of achievement.'

29th: In the train back to Zurich. Greta was right. Despite everything I feel brighter. The scenery affirms. I try to sketch it but fail miserably. Amazing feats of engineering. Like a toy landscape, everything stacked up, layer upon layer. The world is full of mountain, mountain and sky. Trains and cars tootle along the lines and roads, which score the mountain slopes. John would have loved this; John did love this.

The train stops at Airolo, ahead the St Gotthard Pass and tunnel. A middle-aged Scot points out sites to his very young Indian companion. She's immune; I'm glued to the window, sketchpad forgotten. Next stop, Göschenen – walkers, cuckoo clock country, Heidi-land.

An older gentleman, with a suitcase and rucksack, gets on, sits opposite. He looks Swiss, contained and healthy. He smiles, then ignoring the scenery, carefully takes from his rucksack an apple, a checked handkerchief and a red Swiss Army knife. The apple is a bright crisp green; the handkerchief faded with blue and yellow hatching; the knife a Victorinox Climber Swiss Army Knife, code 1370300 VICCLIM, with a small shield. I bought one exactly the same for John.

The gentleman carefully lays the handkerchief across his knees, then he cuts the apple into four. As droplets of juice fall on the cloth, the zing of freshly-sliced Granny Smith wallops my senses; I start to salivate. He peels and cores each segment, neatly. Snakes of green cover the cotton. His fingers are strong and capable. Long fingers, with manicured square, clean nails. The skin is tanned, wrinkled, the veins protrude slightly. These are the hands of an older man.

His hands, the checked handkerchief, the knife. Recognition; time stands still. He is John.

Bill Barich, *Traveling Light*, 1981, Penguin Books.

Seeds and Song

Ouray, Colorado. We stopped for supplies and stayed for five nights. Named after an Indian chief and perched on the San Juan Skyway, Ouray is small town America at its best. Here were hot springs, heritage and hotels. And not another Brit in town.

We changed sterling into dollars, commission-free, the teller never having changed English pounds before.

'Won't ya'all look at the British Queen Elizabeth!' he beamed. Later, although not normally souvenir collectors, we wandered idly into the Clear Mountain gift shop.

'Why do you want a stamp box, John? You never write letters.'

'I just like it,' he replied.

I do too. It lives on the windowsill opposite my desk. Made from auburn-coloured wood, the stamp box is about two inches square. A zig-zag frieze of green, cream and orange dances across the front. Though faded, the colours still glow like windrows of cut corn in sunshine. On one side, there's a slot for stamps, which need to be carefully rolled inside as this is the only opening. On the back, a small heart has been burnt into the wood. Inscribed, the letters are too tiny to read even with a magnifying glass. A worn price tag clings to the bottom. A fine grain skips horizontally across the top, diagonally down the sides. There are no obvious joins, at least none visible. An intriguing object and tactile, slightly perfumed like that of sandalwood. Intriguing – and now doubly precious.

As is the Kokopelli, a silver brooch John bought from nine-year-old Jason.

'Mam,' Jason grinned, shoulders level with the counter top, corn-coloured hair reaching for the sky. 'Can I show you something?'

'Hello, maybe. What's your name?'

'Jason, Mam. What's yours?'

'I'm called Anne. And how old are you?'

'Nine on 15 September. And how old are you, Mam?'

'Thirty-five years older than you,' I replied and we all laughed out loud as his mother emerged from behind a tall stack of t-shirts and yanked his left ear.

Known as a fertility god, prankster, healer and story-teller, Kokopelli embodies the American South West. He dates back over 3,000 years and was a sacred figure to many South Western Indians. In Indian folklore, Kokopelli wanders from village to village with a bag of seeds and songs on his back. He plays songs to melt the winter snows, to usher in spring breezes and warmth, to make the corn grow and maidens fertile.

Buying something from Jason was a must; once the legend understood, Kokopelli was also a given.

My Kokopelli is caught in a Pilates pose, half cat, half camel. Like a silver sprite, he skips through my life with a flute, a bag of seeds and songs. John's stamp box and this Colorado man-child remain a source of comfort and consolation.

Encounter

From Hawthorne we head east
to Rachel, heads fat with UFO yarns,
gouge through cacti, desert scrub
into endless summer, deep Nevada.

Noon: a dust-ball skims the horizon
shades the haze, tumbles closer
in a rhythmic rumble –
movement chills the sands.

The engine coughs, then stalls
heat batters the windscreen
hand grabs hand, hearts stampede;
they watch us, we watch them.

The black stallion rears,
punches at the bonnet
snorts disdain
to comfort his wheeling mares
then gallops them away –
                        leaving us
                              bereft.

Great Sand Dunes

The end of a three-week touring holiday in Colorado, minds like suitcases crammed with memories. Our last day. So many sights and sounds and smells. Almost a surfeit of enjoyment. Time to take in just one more monument before the drive back to Denver.

Majestic, glaring, aloof, the Great Sand Dunes appeared at the end of the San Luis Valley. Constructed from billions of minute particles of sand, they reared to heights of 750 feet, spread over thirty-nine barren square miles. In front of them, like a beach in reverse, a shallow ribbon of cold mountain water.

It was unsettling seeing sand dunes surrounded by dusty cattle grazing on prairies. Everything was out of place. Surely they belonged to the coast, alongside swishing seas, or as a Saharan backdrop to a Bedouin romp? Here they seemed unreal, like a mirage, shimmering in this suffocating heat.

In fact, their origins are less bewitching. They exist simply because, here, all of the essential ingredients came together and allowed nature to create. For centuries, the Rio Grande meandered across the plateau carrying with it sand and sediment. Then the river changed course; massive deposits of sand were exposed to strident winds blowing across the valley, pushing and bouncing sand towards the San Cristo mountains. There, the pummelled fragments found respite. The lighter particles escaped through the passes. The heavier ones, less fleet of foot, remained to form the dunes.

Today the winds still blow, sometimes gently, sometimes at speeds as high as 40 miles an hour. Like relentless Rodins, they shape and reshape the dunes into exotic, sculptured forms. Yet, although each individual dune is highly volatile, together they stand firm and steady, like a well-coached football team. Snows and rains bring minute drops of water, a precious adhesive for the shifting sands. The whole area is often used as a location for alien planet films, but this is no human version of Mars. This is a tough, arid environment where wildlife, with amazing names, has adapted and survives.

The Medano Creek falls from the high country and flows the length of the dunes before disappearing into the sand; it forms a closed basin where the endangered Rio Grande sucker lives, safe from piscatorial predators, as do four types of rare insect found nowhere else on earth. The nocturnal deer mouse shuns daylight hours. The resident kangaroo rat never needs to drink water; he coexists happily with the fantastically named giant sand treader camel cricket. Blowout grass grows beside Indian ricegrass and fragrant scurfpea. In late summer, the luminescent prairie sunflower makes a brief appearance.

We found signs of human life too in the culturally scarred trees, where bark had been peeled from the trunks by Ute Indians for use in waterproofing blankets, in food and in religious ceremonies. And among the trees, we just glimpsed a bobcat. Apparently coyotes, mule deer, elk, rabbits, ravens and magpies also still live here.

The sand dunes are shape-shifters. Not only do they change with the seasons but at different times of the day, light and shadow colour them. We watched soft rose become subtle taupe, glistening cream turn cinnamon, dazzling blue soften into opal. Colours and patterns swirled as if held in the embrace of my kaleidoscope.

There is an old saying in the American National Parks, 'Leave only your footprints behind.' Here, in Colorado, even this was not possible, certainly not for long. For, like memories, our footprints would vanish in the wind.

The Colours of Manassus

Blood red stripes
hard on a confederate sky;
that ever-present flag
slaps and flaps
over Sunday visitors
lunching off the innocent
massacred on Henry Hill.

Deceptive colours, deadly confusion.

Manassus: Virginia battlefield site. Vast numbers of casualties were in
part caused by similar coloured uniforms being worn by the two sides.

Warm Springs

There was something nurturing and gracious about Warm Springs, which reminded us of Ouray.

On Friday we explored. On the way home it started to rain. It rained all night and all day Saturday – warm, soft, sibilant Virginia rain. In the afternoon I sat on the stoop, writing, John was inside dozing. We'd had a bizarre morning.

We'd found the Cascades Gorge with its twelve spectacular waterfalls. Pines, fifty, sixty, seventy feet tall, dwarfed us. Among them were saplings, planted out at regular intervals, their leaves shivering and hissing in the damp atmosphere. Mushrooms grew thickly on the ground, others had formed bulbous growths on fallen branches. Water gurgled over stones in the riverbed, birds were twittering quietly. Then, for no apparent reason, everything went quiet. Dank silence and an all-pervading feeling of dread. At that moment we noticed the hiking trail had been blocked with piles of concrete. We were alone and unwelcome. John grabbed my hand; we left.

With relief we came across the wholesome village of Bacova and the Bacova Gallery, opened in May and still smelling of fresh paint. A smiling lady, wearing a flowered shirtwaister with matching blooms in her hair, welcomed us. Nestled against a hillside surrounded by towering pines, a chapel had been built by hand. It fell into disrepair but was saved by a new owner who restored it.

'He has houses in Warm Springs and Chesapeake Bay, has collected for most of his seventy-six years. He needed a place to show his treasures. This is it.'

A chubby arm swept across the chapel as Denise beamed.

'Even if he sells nothing, he'd still collect and purchase.'

Denise was obviously a fan of the acquisitive 'he.'

'And this is my i–d–e–a–l job.' She spelt out the letters, beaming even more.

Instead of pews and pulpits, the nave was filled with art treasures, on walls, on the floor, on tables: 18th and 19th century paintings, old prints, watercolours, antiques including two German helmets and some attractive local furniture, roughly finished, in dark cherry wood. Soft lighting, reassuringly familiar Scottish music.

That evening we picnicked on the stoop; guests regretted the rain, locals welcomed the end of the drought. And the rain continued, warm and insistent.

Words

I love to read. I love words. I always have. I love everything about them. Their sound: flat, lilting, serious, gay. Their texture: round, bumpy, angular. Their past, their future, their immediacy, the utter connectedness of them all. And their shape, joints that seem to move separately, articulated like the limbs of a favourite doll. Prefixes and suffixes, plaited together into a fat braided sentence, or carelessly scrunched together like a child's bunches. Every colour and shade, blond or brunette, flaming red or ink black. Alone or together they are beautiful. And private. Learning to string words together gave me a world so far removed from my own that, even now, I still feel like crying with the joy of them. Words were, and still are, the land of beauty and imagination, the country of what ifs. Hushed and secret, a place where sentence and phrase are bigger and finer than the words alone, the whole greater than each part. Words are artists. They paint understanding and compassion and love. They colour my world. Words are also like clothes pegs. They can be lined up on the floor. When I was tiny I loved to play with pegs. I would be given the peg-bag, a gaudy thing, half strangled on a coat hanger, covered in spring flowers and pregnant with spiky pegs. I loved pegs before I loved words. I knew them first, you see. Our pegs were tall and thin, with round heads and splayed out legs. They were sweet-smelling and woody. I would line them up, head to toe, dolls camping out. They stretched all the way round the sitting room, right into the kitchen. Off they went, marching one by one, across the thread-bare carpet into the distance, to infinity and beyond. Where they all lived happily ever after.

Angels' Wings

Leaving the ramshackle charms of Oporto behind we headed along the Douro. Up and down, we looped and swooped along picturesque banks. Through Lamego to Parado do Bispo, then up over cobbled hairpins to the Quinta Eufemia – one mile from the river, a 1900s gem in the middle of its own port-producing vineyard.

The senhora greeted us with six dogs in tow – Carmen, Pablo and four belonging to neighbours – then showed us into an immaculate but simple room: two single beds with crochet bedspreads, plain white walls, rugs on the parquet floor, an imposing crucifix on the wall, thick shutters.

We dined in the *quinta* with two other couples, Scots from Edinburgh and Portuguese from Lisbon. Conversation flowed and the food was superb. John was especially taken with the *papoos angelus*, Angels' Wings, a traditional sweet crisp pastry made out of dough, shaped into thin twisted ribbons, deep-fried and sprinkled with powdered sugar. It wasn't the thirteenth, but apparently the tradition here is for husbands to give angels' wings to their wives on Friday the thirteenth to avoid bad luck. I wondered if the opposite applied.

After dinner, port and more wine flowed in the *laga* where we were invited to tread grapes; we trod well into the night.

On Sunday, suffering from an excess of treading, we wandered through the vines with Carmen, then drank restorative beers in the Parado do Bispo bar. Here we were definitely the main attraction. Or was it Carmen?

That afternoon we sunbathed in the vines, reading and sleeping off our beers. With the dog.

'She's very old,' I commented, noting Carmen's sagging belly and wheezing breath.

'I don't think so,' John replied. John was a dog man; he liked dogs and they liked him. 'She's just worn out, had far too many puppies. She should have been sterilised, poor bitch.'

The poor bitch clearly recognised safety. She curled up beside me and we slept, bum to bum. An astonishing event as I am very wary of dogs, anything above ankle height tending to freak me out.

Maybe the *papoos angelus* were already bringing both of us good fortune.

Equivalents

'I am in the beautiful country – our beautiful country ... And oh how I love it. It is really absurd in a way to just love a country as I love this.'
                                                Georgia O'Keeffe

Our tour guide was a Californian, dressed in a sunshine yellow shirt and an antique straw hat. He whistled us around Santa Fe. Such a boho buzz about the place. And – where the light really did ring and sing – the inaugural exhibition at the Georgia O'Keeffe Museum.

Just last year, entranced by her use of colour in massive, reductive flowers, we'd had three prints framed: Light Iris, an abstract eau de nil; White Trumpet Flower, with a strong turquoise backdrop; the enigmatic Green and Blue Music. Here were the originals.

Here too were, not only flowers, but an astonishing variety of subjects: iconic blooms, bleached desert bones, abstractions, nudes, landscapes, city-scapes, still lifes, the 'wideness and wonder of the world' as she lived it.

O'Keeffe often painted fragments, believing they could made a statement as well, or better, than the whole. She created equivalents rather than copies.

The detail in Black Hollyhock Blue Larkspur is one such. We see into the bright heart of the hollyhock, feel the leavening of larkspur. It is a colour poem. Like velvet. Like a saudade, which, in Brazil, means even the saddest thing cannot be so sad that one can never laugh again. Or that the most beautiful thing can ever be so beautiful that one can forget crying.

Auction

Tenho saudades tuas

Lot 1929, ladies and gentlemen
a luscious Georgia O'Keeffe oil on canvas
Black Hollyhock, Blue Larkspur
See the blooms grow, hear their longing.

Three commission bids on this.

I start at Whitby jet, tropical night, anywhere?
On my left, velvet, coal, ebony. Is that a tulip?
On my right, midnight lace, *delphinium parishii*
Am I bid? For loss, for touching absence?

Any advance on royal robes, cornflower,
native bluebells? The lady's bid gentian
hyacinths – sadly forced –
luminous life in MGM technicolour.

An internet bid for deep lake, liquid
darkness, backlit with the colours
of summer, of larks flying free.

Are we all gone? Going, going –

flowers painted by silver fingers
with the authority of sadness
black defies hell, blue soars to heaven –

Gone.

Wash Up

First steps for a novice
shy of showing herself
in that class of prosers
who thought poets posers –
'Can't see why people use poetry to express their hang-ups.'

Afterwards I pondered:
strong emotion or hang-up?
hang-up or hung out to dry?
feelings flowing like water
neither good, nor bad
as neutral as words
sponges we soak
in our stuff.

Years later,
an old travel journal
fat with content
plump with gaps;
weeks after redundancy
yet no sign of anger or sadness
as if they'd been hidden
behind wet washing
while the clothes pole –
uptight and upright –
with wooden optimism
props up the sagging line
one phrase, 'John talked me out of my work hang-ups.'

That word
enough to spin me back
to Logroño
ten thirty at night
the Rioja hot and sultry
smooth tunes
from a boys' brass band

rich cooking smells
tomato, garlic, onions
us on a stone bench
me talking
you listening, uneasily,
to my list –
redundancy, rejection,
reduced, another job
irrelevant –
a flash flood of despair
like taking a talking cure
words releasing grief
setting me free.

Olio Piccante come Fuoco

October 1993, my forty-fifth birthday, the *Route des Grandes Alpes.*

'Five hundred and sixty five kilometres from Lake Geneva to the Mediterranean. A fantastic road through unbelievable scenery. Some of the passes are obstructed by snow between October and May.' The AA Europe Road Book doesn't mention rain and storms.

'We'll manage,' I told John, who frowned slightly, wrinkling his nose. Even his glasses looked startled.

Somewhere off Cherbourg our continental breakfast ended up in my handbag, permanently foxing our passports. It was bitterly cold. And wet. It was bitterly cold and wet all the way to Mont Blanc – past Lake Geneva, round Thonon-les-Bains, through the Gorges de la Drause and du Diable and at Les Gets, at Morzine-Avoriez, at Sallanches.

Finally we floated into Chamonix, where a beaming Irishman welcomed us with the widest of open arms and the hottest of hot towels. The Hotel du Midi was warm and dry; like walking into toast.

And the next day clear, blue skies. Mont Blanc towered above Chamonix like a dream. It was too windy for the Aiguille du Midi cable car to operate so we took the rack and pinion railcar to Montenvers, cold, misty and marvellous. We lunched in a noisy pizzeria, a colourful Regina and a sunny Margherita, both fired up with red hot chilli-flavoured oil.

October 2009, sixteen years later. Courmayeur, 1224 metres, a large winter sports resort, tucked under Mont Blanc in Italy high above the valley of Aosta. Through the tunnel lie France and Chamonix.

I'd caught the bus up from Aosta. Mist over the mountains; it was raining. Courmayeur in October is pants (does this feel familiar?), even the church is called after San Pantalone. The Alpine Guide Museum is closed from noon until three thirty. I search for traces of Albert Smith. In 1851, Smith, a journalist and entertainer, reached the top of Mont Blanc with three Oxford students and sixteen guides. He was not the first though; in 1786 two Chamonix natives had climbed the mountain. Apparently the said Smith had an exhibition here in one of the side streets. That's closed too, either for the season or for lunch. I decide to follow suit, slush my way back to the pizzeria on the square.

I open the door, my glasses steam up, I turn to walk out. This is no pizzeria but a heaving sauna, stuffed like oversized ravioli, with loud, gesticulating French brats. Though the boys and girls sit separately, they eat for France, each and every pea-stick of them. Four adults supervise from a separate table. The padrone bustles over.

'Sì, sì signora. C'è una tavola. Ecco qua! Tutto bene.'

The noise is like an avalanche. At home I'd have vamoosed. Yet here I'm amused and comforted by French after weeks of struggling with Italian. All helped along by some gutsy red wine and a fourteen-inch Regina. Plus litre bottles of oil flavoured with thyme, rosemary and red hot chilli peppers. A bitter-sweet experience. The *olio piccante come fuoco* was doing the rounds, connecting us through that love of food, which is so much a part of the Italian love of life. A nod from one of the teachers and Jean le Beau swaggers over.

'Grazie, benissimo,' I say.

For a minute he looks surprised, then smiles.

Suddenly everything seems bellissimo. Everything is -issimo. Issimo! I pull out a scrap of paper, start tinkering around with the suffix, run out of paper. The host brings me another.

'È poeta? Incredibile!' He beams, belts out, 'Ecco la signora. È poeta.'

In the roar of his *poeta* possibility simmers, a tiny inkling of probability, the prospect of a kinder identity. Perhaps I can become a poet, as well as a proser, rather than a lonely widow, longing for what can never return.

Chilli Peppers

My niece plops thyme, garlic
and three red chilli peppers
into pure virgin oil, then stirs
and bottles for Christmas:
months later the Alps
blaze through my kitchen –
as hot and feisty
as hope.

Iceberg

Summer 1999. Bergen, Norway. We decided to take a day trip. We were such gluttons for travel-punishment that year. I now wonder if subliminally we were running from what was to come – or were we like lemmings heading straight for it?

From Dragsvik we took the ferry to Hella, then pottered along the Sognefjorden past power lines hung low like sagging clothes lines across the fjord, to the fruit-producing area around Leikanger. At Solvorn, an ancient local sold us ice creams; we chatted in the sunshine beside cottages that were spilling into the harbour. It was warm and peaceful; we were too. After lunch at the Breheimsenteret Glacier and Adventure Centre, we climbed the Nigardsbreen, said to be the most beautiful tongue of the Jostedalsbreen fjord.

The road ran through some strange moraine landscape to a lake at the foot of the Jostedalsbreen Glacier, the largest in mainland Europe. A motorboat took us to the ice floe. We'd never been up close to a glacier before. It was macabre. Not bright white, but a dirty eau de nil. Not particularly cold either. Folded and pitted, with crevasses and seracs and craters, all caused by weight stress, the glacier creaked and groaned and moaned. It felt malevolent.

We could have turned back, but the road continued, so we continued too. We climbed, the automatic grumbling through its gears, up to the Styggevatn Dam, 60 metres high, 850 metres wide, 1220 metres above sea level. A massive sign, *Beware of Icebergs.* Two had calved in the reservoir waters; they lurked, ready to attack.

That evening the Bryggenstuen & Bryggenloftet is hot and noisy. We wait for a table, then for dinner. Steaming elk steaks hurry by. We choose elk and reindeer, less squeamish about eating Santa's friends than the week before. We sip red wine. John looks pale. Eventually dinner arrives. John takes one mouthful and passes out. He seems to crumple inwards. Wine and food crash to the floor. His face is on the table. Everyone stops talking. Utter silence. In an instant I am beside him, my heart careering.

'John, Johns.' I have no idea what to do.

He comes to, shouts out as if he's been hurt, loudly in the silent tavern.

'Where am I? What's happening?' He is petrified.

'In a restaurant. In Norway. It's OK. You blacked out. It must be the heat.'

The waitress hovers. Another comes over with a damp cloth, some cold water. She offers to call a doctor; we settle for a taxi. Outside, his colour returns.

'I think the day was a bit much,' he grins. 'Don't worry.' He smiles. 'I'm just tired.' He might as well have said stop breathing. How to stop worrying?

Back at the hotel, he lies down, goes straight to sleep. I lie awake listening to his breathing, ready to act if it changes. Ready for anything that might happen. I lie awake until 4.00 am, hear the church clock chime each hour. The room is long and thin, like a corridor, with two single beds placed head to toe. We sleep head to head, like bodies laid out. The wallpaper is green. I can see that room now; I can feel that long, black night in that long, thin room.

In the morning John feels better, although, in the afternoon, he has a giddy turn. That evening at the Bryggenstuen & Bryggenloff we are greeted like long-lost friends. John eats elk: I eat reindeer.

Back in the UK John underwent tests; nothing untoward was detected. But I was left with a niggling sense that something was wrong. I have a tendency to catastrophise, to add two and two and make seven. In my mind this blackout started to merge with a panic attack John had had when driving in Denver. A burly policeman had led us back to the hotel. Yet Denver isn't complicated; it's a grid, a grid where every street looks the same.

Tragically, I wasn't catastrophising. Both were signs of the vascular dementia that was lurking, like the icebergs behind the Styggevatn Dam, ready, waiting.

Chautara

Hillier Gardens

They've built a terraced garden
from Nepalese plants and cultivars –
a gentle *namaste.*

We travelled there together –
chattering prayer wheels
shy smiles under Topi hats
feisty flags, Kathmandu-calm.
Our Sherpa drove us north
across scree plains, into the hills.
'Aye – aye, my car,' he cried
but still we climbed
towards kukri peaks.

Here,
a string of ponds linked by a bamboo walkway, a bridge over
knotweed, dinner plate poppies, ginger, a giant mountain lily.

Next,
a dry stone wall and a dusty river bed loop round the slope
where *Bholua Gurkha* flowers beside Himalayan white birch.

Finally,
the *chautara,* open to the sky, its walls guarding sacred trees –
Banyan and Pipal share the weight of memory.

Namaste.

Chautara: Traditional Nepalese resting place, often a memorial to a
loved one.

In the Beginning

Your Boys' Brigade Bible
badly bound in crimped leatherette
with impractical fluted edges
that curl over foxed gold leaf;
on the front a faded crest,
an anchor with two words –
sure and *stedfast.*

Inside,
'Awarded to Pte John Sherry
The Bible Class Prize, 1945';
Cpt. Cyril Bedwell's fading copperplate
whispers of *Peace in Europe*
and the columns of tissue text
rustle *Butler boy, Baptist born.*

I stroke the crinkled, grey leather
massage bath oil into the cracks
lavender and must,
imagine the words heavy
in a grubby, twelve-year-old hand,
feel the need of a quirky boy
for his damp-fold friend.

'Stedfast' has been modernised to 'steadfast' in recent years but, for
authenticity, I prefer the original at it appears on John's bible.

Paint it Black

Difficult – and very distressing – to recall much that I deliberately erased. Yet, as I write of that time, the feelings experienced then – pain, disbelief and anger – return through the words. Frustration, conflict and confusion leak from the prose. Like picking at an old scar. Or deliberately recalling love-run-amok. If happiness writes white, these pages paint black.

At first, there were tiny changes, niggling actions that jarred, as if concrete blocks in a dam wall were subtly shifting. Nothing as ominous as the blackout, but destabilising. And eventually, very annoying.

Christmas shopping in Reading. As we enter John Lewis John suddenly says. 'I like Welwyn Garden City.'

'Why did you say that?' I ask.

'Because we're there,' he replies.

John had been brought up in Welwyn Garden City. I guessed he was conflating the two John Lewis stores.

The dishwasher malfunctions. Being an engineer John loved dismantling and fixing things. In a hotel he'd always try to repair a broken table lamp rather than ask reception to change it.

I come home from a meeting; dishwasher parts are strewn over the utility room floor. John is watching TV, something he never does during the day.

'What's going on? When are you going to put it back together?' I ask.

'I'll do it later,' he answers, but doesn't. We dump the dismembered dishwasher.

We have an old fax machine with paper on a roll. It works as long as a fax isn't too long. Someone sends through twenty pages. I arrive home; a streamer of fax paper runs from the study, down the stairs and into the hall. The house is a parody of the toilet roll advert.

'Why didn't you pick it up?' I ask crossly.

'I didn't want to mess things up,' comes the reply.

It is as if my helpful, ever-there-for-me partner is on sabbatical. Or he's given up.

By this time I'd left Seagram and was working independently. I asked John to keep the accounts as he'd always been the numerate one.

When we first met, long before computers, I was a junior personnel officer struggling with figure work. John happily took over the production of Zenith Carburetter's labour turnover statistics.

'Anne, your figure work has improved enormously,' my boss declared.

It hadn't; it never did. I was the one who scraped through O level maths, the one who could never do percentages until John taught me how.

Now John muddles up the accounts, leaves them in a heap on the dining room table.

'There's no rush,' he says.

I end up sorting four months' figures the night before the accountant comes to collect them. Meanwhile John watches TV, then goes to bed.

The cleaner leaves.

'I'll do it,' John says.

He doesn't. The house is filthy. I find another cleaner.

'John's bored,' says my father.

'Well, John needs to do something,' I retort. I vividly remember thinking: I'm not a cash cow. I didn't mind John not working. I could and wanted to earn enough for our needs. I did care if he did nothing.

'You need to find some interests,' I say. 'It's unhealthy just hanging around.' I recalled John saying something similar to his brother, David who, after retirement, just sat and stared at the wall. David, who has Alzheimer's.

We buy a keyboard. John starts a class but doesn't practise. We sell the keyboard.

My father gives John his wood-turning lathe. Two months later it follows the keyboard.

In the study, one late afternoon. I'm struggling with the printer. Technology, like maths, is not my thing. This was one of the days when that tiny study felt like a coffin. John barges in and asks how he should cut up the courgettes for our evening stir-fry.

My reply is not ladylike.

'It's as if he's disconnected from reality,' I confide in a girlfriend.
'I wonder if you should talk to his doctor,' she suggests.

I, on the other hand, am fully connecting – with my darker side. I lose my temper. I am irritable. Some days I sound like a fishwife. The more I nag, the less John does. The less he does, the more I nag. My going away on business gives us respite; my being at home further enflames marital discord. Amazing that I manage to hold down even one consultancy contract. John is changing and this is changing me too. I dislike the new me even more than I dislike the new John. Unreasonable behaviour has gate-crashed our lives.

When I stop to think I can see the fundamental differences in John. As if black has become white; white black. But I don't often give myself that luxury. I'm in full business start-up mode, half running the house, trying to keep a lid on the tension between us. And each and every day, I'm subconsciously mourning John. And not understanding.

Much later – when we stopped fighting – John confessed he didn't think I'd like working independently. He himself had hated it. I, on the other hand, loved being my own boss. And keeping busy allowed me to ignore the loss of the lovable, old John; to confront what was happening to us.

Then our beloved black cat, Welly (aka Wellington Boot) loses his faculties and is put down.

Another loss.

John sees the doctor, starts a course of anti-depressants.

During the winter of 2000/2001 we have twelve sessions with Relate. It helps, but doesn't solve the fundamental problem. Our needs and wants are opposed. John had hoped my working from home would mean us spending more time together; in fact spending more time together became a problem. I'd hoped John would become more active through helping me with the business; by then he had neither the inclination, nor the capacity, to do so.

'Dementia leads to a lack of motivation,' the memory psychiatrist later told me.

I wish I could plot a definite time line. I'd like to paint the whole sequence, like a clever little case-study: when this happened, when that happened, what do you think followed? and what might the end result have been? But in the real world there's no one point when a relationship changes, no absolutely clear link between cause and effect.

What is ice-clear though is that when I worked from home I realised how little John did to stimulate his mind, that he did change in increasingly more significant ways and that the dementia was developing – in Denver, in Norway – long before it was officially diagnosed. It was there all along; it just wasn't recognised. I still beat myself up for not realising. But I wasn't alone. Dementia is often mistaken for, and treated as, depression because the early symptoms of one mimic the other.

Once we had brought out the best in each other. Now we were bringing out the worst. Deep down we still loved one another. It was precisely because we wanted that love to survive that we went semi-detached. Continuing to live together was no longer an option.

Semi-Detached

Fragment 1

We return to the surgery. More tests. Doctor Ingram asks about the Sherry family history, recommends a brain scan, a memory psychologist. He looks concerned when John mentions his father's senile dementia, his brother's Alzheimer's.

'How are you?' I ask as we leave.

'Oh dear, Annie,' he replies. 'Pretty scared. But it's you I'm worried about. I don't want to get like my brother and have you put up with that. Look at Marion. She looks twenty years older than she is.'

I feel sick, worn out for my sister-in-law, Marion. What to say for the best?

'If it happens we'll handle it together. Anyway the scan could be months away. Let's talk to Marion. You seeing Di helps. And I'm going back to Martin.' (Di was our Relate counsellor; Martin my therapist.)

At last it feels as if there is some support for both of us.

'I'll look after you, you know that, but I won't stay home to do it. I'd go crazy. I'm too young, too driven. It would be financially disastrous.' And, I think, we'd end up driving one another crazy.

In the kitchen he says, 'Give me a cuddle. I need it.'

We both do. A long, bear hug. Am I saying the right things? Doing the right thing? We are both in free fall now.

Over dinner John says, 'It's pretty grim, Annie. Awful for me, but in a way, it's worse for you. You don't know what I'm going to come out with next, do you?'

'I love you,' I say. 'I always have.'

His 'Thank God' comes from deep. We are both screwed up inside, raw with emotion.

I run a training course for Carlsberg in Copenhagen. John comes for the weekend, gets lost at the airport. The results of the brain scan arrive, everything normal. I am offered work with Diageo on the Seagram portfolio. I feel sick, refuse the assignment. John loses his temper, throws a glass across the kitchen, sobs in the garden. Five minutes later he's laughing. I envy him being able to forget, feel ashamed of my thoughts.

One happy day. A heron flies over the garden, lands on the neighbour's wall. John watches from his workshop, smiling, I watch him watching the heron.

In June we look at a flat for sale in Camberley. It is small, freshly painted, with pleasant grounds. John likes it.

'Nice, Annie,' he says. 'Clean.' Then as we get to the car 'Who's going to live there?'

My head spins, my ears pop. I hold on to the Saab, rest my forehead on the silver roof, say quietly, 'John, the plan was for you to live there.'

'I live with you.'

'You do not. You're in a rented flat. We agreed we'd try living apart.' And enough finally becomes enough. 'John, I can't go on like this. You're ruining my life. And my health. If I'm ill who'll look after you?'

Tears well up in his eyes. Someone has to make the decision. This can't go on. I take his hand.

'We'll sell the house and get two flats next to one another.'

'I want a house.'

'What for? We might not be able to afford a house. And you'll forget to look after it.'

Back at his flat, the purple lounge is full of washing; it feels like home.

Unravelled

I'm unravelling
Kn.1,p.1, kn.2tog

I'm a heap of used yarn
a loopy soup of short endings
once knitted art, with broken rib
mock cable, French knots
worked in reversed-out plain
now a mess of bobbled hopes.

I'm unravelling
Kn.1,p.1, kn.2tog

Help me
      find a pattern
help me
      knit myself together again.

Fragment 2

In July we attend the Memory Clinic at Frimley Park Hospital. We only saw this particular psychiatrist once. I imagined her on secondment to the UK.

Dr Lidia Martis is an eccentric delight, a psychologist on assignment from Jung's consulting rooms. Her skin is pale. Her hair is arranged in a kind of droopy French pleat, horizontal rather than vertical, with two fierce brown grab clips at the back. Her stockings – they cannot have been tights – were wrinkled at the ankles and covered in the sort of woolly bobbles we used to pull off jumpers and make into cooties when we were children. As she talks gently to John I have a sudden desire to crawl on the floor and pick them off her legs. Her shoes are sensible lace-ups. Her baggy suit is olive green with buttercup petal cut-outs around the hems of skirt and jacket. She wears gold-framed glasses, a chunky male wristwatch, a pale blue power stone bracelet and a brass brooch in the shape of a squashed tiger. She is a prime candidate for *Ten Years Younger*.

She asks about John's family, listens gravely as John recounts how his father beat him with a riding crop until it broke. She asks about his childhood, his mother, our relationship, notices his trembling hands.

'No John, don't look at your wife, look at me.'

She asks permission to do a little test. This is the Mini-Mental State Examination, which I will grow to love and fear in equal measure. The MMSE is a simple test, which measures a person's memory capability on that particular day. There are about fifteen simple questions. Where are we? Which floor are we on? Where is the hospital? Today's date? What is going on in the world? Spell 'world' backwards. Count one to ten backwards. And always three words – such as bear, apple, chair – to be remembered after two further questions have been asked (John never managed to remember the three words). There is a line drawing to be copied. A piece of paper to be taken with one hand and folded with the other – apparently a neurologically complex task. A person with no memory problems would easily score thirty out of thirty. On 20 July, John scores twenty-four.

Gentle and placid, she reminds me of a cow, ruminating on the cud of memory loss. But her last question is fully focussed.

'How did you keep your soul intact with that sort of childhood? Especially a man?'

We return to the Memory Clinic in August, still twenty-four out of thirty. And again, in September.

'What exactly is wrong? Is it dementia?' I ask Dr Warner.

'Yes, it is mild dementia.'

'And is there any cure?' I ask, naïve and ignorant. 'Anything to be done?'

'There are tablets we can try.'

She prescribes a three months supply of Aricept privately. They cost one hundred pounds.

John dents his Peugeot. Black under-paint seeps though the diablo red.

'I don't care,' he mutters.

I mention sheltered accommodation, thinking short-term this would be safer. Then I can sell the house, find two conjoined flats.

'I'm not ready for that. The thought makes me ill.' He retches. 'I won't go into one of those places.'

I see my reflection in an Oxfam shop window. I look like a bag lady.

John's cousin Pam calls. I tell her we have separated for a while, that things are better, about the dementia. No judgement.

'It's your lives; you live them, nobody else,' she says. 'You'll find out who your real friends are now.'

In October John scores twenty-seven. Dr Warner is euphoric, bouncing up and down in her seat. She is, if possible, even nicer than Dr Martis.

'Well, well, well done, John!'

We both beam at him; he beams back.

Old Flame

Trousers knock-kneed on a bent wood chair
small change, a leather wallet, Polo mints
your Swiss Army penknife, one black button.

You look the same, still gentle, an older you
but time has reworked your mind, a pendulum
that swings, to and fro, to and fro
through twisted cogs, scorched synapses.

Regret gouges deep, bloody
as the blade on your old chain saw;
I only learnt to love you again
when disease had burnt you away.

Fragment 3

I get a call from Shaftesbury Housing Association. A place has unexpectedly become available at Wimborne House in Farnborough.

John and I visit on a Monday afternoon, meet Corinne, the chain-smoking Scheme Manager.

'You do your own thing. I don't look after the tenants,' she glowers at John.

'Fine. Can I see it?' He smiles.

A tenant walks into the office, without knocking. 'Here's the money from the raffle, Corinne,' she says. 'Hello.' She peers over twisted spectacles at John.

'Are you looking at number 26? Good. Do you want to see mine? There's furniture in it. Looks better.'

Amy's flat is small, one large room, with the bed part-hidden through an arch, a separate kitchen and bathroom. It feels snug, safe.

We all take the lift to the second floor. Two windows look out over a large lawn, backed by a rhododendron wood, a weathered bird table half hidden among the lustrous leaves. A small jet flies over; we are close to the airfield.

'I used to work in the aviation industry,' John tells Corinne. 'I'll feel at home here. I'll take it.'

'Are you sure?' I ask. Of course it's me that isn't sure. 'You don't want to think about it?'

'No, I'm sure. There's a lovely view and the people are nice.' He looks at Corinne and Amy.

The next step is to arrange a home visit to check that John can manage alone. I talk to the office in Salisbury. Now I push; I push hard. I'm scared he'll change his mind, or that Corinne will, or that I will, or that he'll fail the home visit. I've started consulting my horoscope, read that a breakthrough is imminent.

Though I'm working with Barclays, my mind is totally focussed on 26 Wimborne House. I can't call Salisbury again. I've called twice since Monday. My palms are sweating, another hot flush coming on.

The phone rings.

Is that Mrs Sherry? Shaftesbury Housing here. Mr Sherry has the flat. Corinne says a home visit isn't necessary. He'll fit in well. Mrs Sherry, are you still there?'

My throat seizes up. I cough to hide my tears. We agree to take the flat on 17 December, move John in on 1 January 2002. My brother and sister-in-law offer to help; Colin and Kay, at this time, before, after, during and since, my much-loved bridge over trouble water.

John's son and daughter throw a party for his seventy years. A bit like setting out high tea on the *Titanic*, I think sourly, appreciating the gesture yet despairing at the timing.

Dan, a National Service chum, comes with his wife Caroline; they too are living semi-detached.

Cousin Pam is also there. She's squatting awkwardly on a low designer stool. I squat down beside her.

'You'll get used to being alone in the house.' She looks around step-daughter Linda's dez rez. 'Especially as your house isn't as big as this.'

'Or nearly as chic' I grin.

'Not even shabby chic,' she adds.

We laugh happily together.

'What are you two gossiping about?' cousin John yells. Husband John ignores us.

Pam continues. 'Life's hard when you're a child. And sometimes it's even worse when you grow up.'

I nod.

'So what's it all about, Anne? What counts?'

'How about precious cousins you connect with?'

Pam kisses me.

Purple

prose, passion, power
hearts, mourning.

I see you tall
against a Dorset sky
lilac, amethyst, gashed violet.

Cloud fingers your cheek
sketches your nose
mists you mauve.

I search your eyes – gauzy
confusion refracts my rage
my useless love.

Grey

gun metal, pewter, smoke
gravestones, grief.

Hungerford Bridge stabs at the vapid sky
slashes the clouds with fine black lines.

Yesterday I emptied the Peugeot –
your red fleece still jaunty in the boot –
diablo red scrunched to oblivion,
written off like the mess in your head.

I'm still today, in respite, winter pale
dull as the glimmer from our dead star.

.

Siena Mourning

Bellissimi!
Verdi, Callas and Cole
massage memories across il Campo
towards the pizzeria, where we wait
for Margherita, Romana, Calabrese.

Narrow back-streets, wrought iron
against time-sanded stone, terraces,
so many perfect restaurants –
at ease in the loose-fitting comfort
of an always thing.

Across that field of remembrance
I see Sirmione:
watch you feed pizza crusts
to the swans below the palazzo walls
ungrateful, they beak your knees
while I, cowardly soul,
hide behind the pontoon and laugh
you laugh too, playing the fool
my fool.

You'd be proud of me now
I'm less of a coward;
it's just the laughing
that might take longer.

Cowardly soul: Inspired by Emily Brontë, *No Coward Soul Is Mine*,
1848.

Skydive

In aid of the Alzheimer's Society

Salisbury Plain, February 2004.

Warm gloves, orange jumpsuit
harness, helmet, goggles.
The look? Jaffa sausage.
'No, you don't need insurance
just keep out of the instructor's way.'
Hah!
Not so easy when you're strapped together.
'And never grab his hand
he needs it more than you.'
Wanna bet?

Sherry and Costello! To the plane!

A wooden step, up into the lozenge
two skydivers wide, tandems last
slotted together on the floor
tums to bums, legs like chevrons
up close and extremely personal.
The Cessna trundles around rabbit holes
then rises like yeast, circles
and climbs plumb over Stonehenge.
Jane winks at me;
my eyes mist, my lip trembles.
She gives me a thumbs-up;
I feel thumbs down.

One last loop, the door opens;
at fourteen thousand feet
solos shoot out –
Bang! Bang! Bang! –
like shots from a sawn-off.
I've changed my mind.
Wayne and I shuffle up

umbilically joined;
the Cessna throbs, bored.
Next!
Jane tips out;
she's silently screaming
or is that me?
Now I can see the jumpmaster
clinging on outside
a malevolent monkey with a camera
ready to pounce.
Is that only sweat I feel?

My mind blanks as the world ends.

Wind screams,
thick noise, thin light.
I taste cloud, metal
the skies howl with me.
Head up, head down
nowhere, everywhere
ankles crossed, legs curved
arms folded
head pinned to his 3000-jump chest
a middle-aged Icarus pretending to fly
pre-verbal baby whimpers blown away
in the tilting, twisting
that drags us to earth
at one twenty miles an hour.

The sky darkens, backs crack –
they call it the *knacker cracker* –
then pale blue unfurls above
and – Miracle! – we slow   to   still,
float   hushed.
Ears thud, heart thrums, soul aches
arms flop, frosted
minus twenty degrees.
'OK?'

I bleat
'Shall we do a turn?'
I whimper
'Still OK?'
Arms useless, frozen flapping.
'Hold the harness.'
I *would* have preferred his hand.

But we are calm now, serenely rocking backwards and forwards
up and down towards Figheldean, back to Woodhenge, east, west,
north, south, waltzing with the wind that rocks the baby, strapped
to its mother, a pastel quilt below, soft green and creamy beige, a
world of Lego blocks and Dinky toys.

'Lift your legs.'
'Pardon?'
I drift back to this cold here, this sour now.
'Lift your legs up, out of the way,
if you try to walk you'll break an ankle.'
I grunt.
'I'll do the landing;
trust me I'm a skydiving instructor.'
His smile warms the back of my neck
as gravity yanks my legs down.

And so the wicked fairy's castle
looms closer, Netheravon army base,
littered with collapsed divers
crumpled chutes, a lemon truck
and two white faces
pinched with reflected anxiety
coming ever clooooooser.
A scramble of legs
then I'm grabbed, held,
supported, kissed.
'You did it!'

For an hour after

my legs won't stop trembling
and my body shakes
as the malevolent monkey
pours sugar into hot tea
writes out my certificate
gives me a video
and a photograph.

Is that *me* hanging on a cloud?

Red

blood, curse, holly bearing berries;
danger, rage.

Yesterday the cops found your car
straddled along the crash barrier;
I phone around, get it sorted,
joke about next time, gag
wear the face of a clown.

Today they report a woman
spilt over, *ras le bol,*
who dumped her man
at the local hospital.
'You share the load,' she screamed.

No fun, one doing for two
where two once did for one.

White Nights

Midnight, snow falling
a train spits down the track:
sparklers for Christmas
your hand cold in mine.

3.00 am, a broken mould:
scraps of wax, papier maché
macramé lace, pearls, feathers
silver glitter, Murano glass
and round, blank eye holes.

Daybreak, the towpath
dreich, grizzling:
a white arc gleams down
wide wings ride the grey.

Headland

This year closes sadly
softly grey
like mist
on that headland
where a week ago
I sat, high and alone,
bullied by Atlantic gusts
back into this life.

Tonight as I watch
the year fade
eager for colour
to brighten this vanishing time
I stride that mean
high water line
across Fistral beach
slither over mussel-crusted rocks
scream with the gulls –
attuned.

Travel Writing with Alex

Playing truant in the Lot
on a hot hillside
under acrylic skies.

Lush vines snake
over the horizon, slither
past stubbed cornfields;
poplars punctuate the view
stand tall behind ruched tiles
where house martins nest.

A lime butterfly, trailing
scents of passionflower,
tantalises my tongue;
distant, *doucement*
a sleepy cockerel crows
as a *Deux Chevaux* backfires.

Noonday sun, soft on eyelids.

I doze
hear conversations
murmurs of might-have-been
whispered hopes
feel the scratch of conscience
fragments of a life.

A slight breeze rustles leaves,
two tap, crisp together
one falls. I look up –
branch becomes view –
a definite, black stroke
summoning me back to work.

Blue

blood, berries, babies
broke heart blues.

A coal black fortnight
gritty with unwept tears
one crisis bleeds into the next
three-dimensional confusion
repetition to deafen a soul –
tonight I'm the one dementing,
can't face your Christmas Fayre.

You ring, I tense.

'I bought a book –
a lovely history book –
they let us choose –
before the Fayre –
with pictures –
only three pounds,
just what I need.'

You need more
than a history book, my love;
I'd buy you a library
if it sorted your mind.

'Reparation' says the Therapist

I know the word, of course
just not this context;
it sounds so adult
unyielding
a thinking thing.
I look it up in the thesaurus:
atonement bellows out
at one ment, unity,
amend sounds mean
like a string of empty sorrys,
compensation doesn't fit either
too much a payoff,
I cringe at *restitution,*
repair feels better
more kindly, compassionate.

A benign man
somehow ageless
gently tends a torn rag doll
replaces lost buttons
patches tears
darns her soul
stitches her whole.
He doesn't try to make her new
just hems each frayed edge
finds the exact filling to replace
the old that trickled away
like sand from a cracked timer
gritty with unwept tears.

Maybe *renewal* works best.
I must ask what you think;
we like words, we two.

Relative Values
For Brenda Lealman

Here they are again, lined up on that wet, old wall
the buckled steel one resembling a crash barrier;
and, if one of those blighters should accidentally fall
or
      if I push hard enough
               push as hard as hell?

The first bottle's wearing chintz
with a cloche hat, neat, closed-in
forties style with an inky scent
inherited from hubby, the Scribe.

The Pharisee in a frock –
'New Agers are devil worshippers' –
prays we might stay together –
is God skilled at ungluing synapses?

The third, too fat to get through the eye
of anything, finds our house 'big enough'
repetition on the golf course 'too much';
'it comes with the devil,' I say.

Pebble Dash, a *whitened sepulchre,*
loathes 'darkies,' believes in
a wife's duty to stimulate her man,
never takes meals with tax-dodgers.

The blond China doll forgets
'you're family now,' disapproves
'not a proper marriage,' never
says sorry, even on the Sabbath.

In the gloom of my autumn gloaming, ten green bottles
glimmer, eery-peery they stare at me from the past;
five stay schtum as hat, frock, golfer, tomb and blond hair

start a-shimmy and a-shake. The wall shrugs like a sodden
great Saint Bernard, then – Crash! All fall down!
No green bottles hanging on the wall.

Brenda

Such a deep calm about her
      refined, all slightly at odds
           with that relapsed flapper style.

I ask for facts, preferably New Testament,
      none of that blood 'n guts Job stuff,
         bonnes bouches to beef up my *oeuvre*

We end up talking
      about you, our separation and,
         of course, by-the-book green bottles

'And where was love?' she asks
      'you clearly cared or you'd have walked
         but …?'

I'm curious about the Nazarene she describes
      a man with the soul of a poet –
         another user of words to free literal minds.

Jeanne

Walking, sedately but with significant purpose, across this swathe of broken glass Jeanne Berndt entered our lives. With her came a Scrabble-set in search of players and a chic French handbag stuffed with powerful caring instincts and a lifetime's experience. Jeanne became the adjunct to our marriage; she helped us deal with the dementia devil; she also became my friend.

Born Eugénie Mauger in June 1922 to a family of goldsmiths and engravers – her great great grandfather fled to England during the French Revolution – Jeanne was the youngest of two daughters. She spent the war years in the Land Army, continuing 'to work in the greenhouses in Hertfordshire' after the war. It was here that she met and, in 1948, married her German husband, a POW taken captive during the bombing of Dresden. This must have taken some courage; I imagine anti-German feeling was still strong. I remember my father's ill-concealed dislike for my new German friend in 1970 and this was *twenty-two* years after the war.

'I was unhappy for years,' Jeanne says. 'He wasn't gentle, like John. Not a gentleman. Everything I did was wrong. My solicitor was so angry.'

She divorced him in 1972.

'The relief. I can still feel the relief.' She sighs, settling back into John's wing back armchair.

'It was such a difficult time.'

By 1978, her two daughters had left home.

'I felt stuck, my life a mess,' she confides.

So, again showing great courage and resilience, at age fifty-six, this conventional, Christian lady decided to go abroad, to Jerusalem.

'I had two jobs, both voluntary. The first, in Nazareth, was at St Margaret's Home for Handicapped Children, both Arab and Israeli. Later, I moved to a home for older people in Haifa, again Arab and Israeli. The Arabs had to convert to be admitted.' She pauses.

'Many had Alzheimer's. I started in the kitchens, but they were so short of nurses they made me into an auxiliary. Pushed me in at the deep end, couldn't see the bottom.'

She laughs with delight.

'There was always a trained nurse on call but I gave out medications, injections – things that would never have been allowed in the NHS. My daughter, by then a qualified nurse, was horrified. One poor dear had a colostomy. Left her with a big hole in her side. I had to deal with the daily waste. I felt so humbled being able to do this. It was a special time. Israel was lovely. The warmth, the friendship. A bit like Wimborne House. This was the time of my life. I only returned when I started getting terrible migraines, had to take days off at a time.' She looks sad.

Back in the UK Jeanne again worked in residential care, retiring and moving to Wimborne House four years before John.

One summer day we sit and talk together. John has gone to see the Scheme Manager.

'He's not so good this week, a bit shaky,' Jeanne comments.

'Why do you look after John?' I ask. 'You're so good with him. You don't have to, you know. We could always sort out a care package; we'll manage somehow.'

'God led me to him,' she says simply. 'My older sister died of cancer and I wasn't able to do much as my girls were so young. John and I have become friends; I'm happy to do what I can. He is such a lovely man; funny and easy and grateful. And you are always there. It is so worthwhile.'

'I'm glad we are friends,' I say.

'I am too Anne, delighted doesn't cover it.'

We sit happily together as we often do when John is with us. In the way he always is.

Later, I reflect that, like faith and hope, love can appear in many guises. And that the greatest of the three is, indeed, love.

Sundays, Prague

Sometimes, just sometimes, life gives you what you need, when you need it. It doesn't happen often. Life gave me Prague when I needed her – in the form of a sixty-day contract, later much extended.

My journal notes are fractured, disjointed, negative. Yet, the words I write later ping off the page with *joie de vivre*, like the stature of the girl in *Náměstí Míru*. I wonder if there's something here about stories – the stories we tell others, the stories we tell ourselves, the stories our memory concocts. There's clearly not one truth, but different versions of a truth.

Sundays were days to reflect, to call John.

9ᵗʰ February: Here I feel OK being alone. It suits me. I've grown into it. At home in Farnborough solitude hangs off me like a baggy, old dressing gown. Maybe I'm like Kafka, not allowed to remain too long in one place. 'There are people who can acquire a sense of home only when travelling.'
16ᵗʰ February: Suffering profound, painful ambivalence about John. On the phone he's forgetful, vague, dependent. My feelings are strong, angry. But we still laugh together.
'You always say men are horrible.'
'They are. They think they're always right. They're not. I know I'm not. I don't care. He! He! When I sit and think of my life I'm amazed at all the places I've been to, and it's largely thanks to you, so I'm really grateful.'
'But we did go together.'
'I know, but that's what I wanted to say.'
This closeness in the distance between us is reassuring, like appreciation from afar. At other times he's so hurtful, curt, offhand. Like a different person.
22ⁿᵈ February: A lazy day. Quiet music from another flat. Sunshine, the warm balcony, a jasperware sky. My mind full of my landlady Kristina's words, 'As many languages as a man speaks so he is that many men.' Different worlds within different languages, worlds within words.

John, still himself, despite that robber of memories. I always had this fear of him growing old; when the fear disappeared something else happened.

Milton was right: 'The mind is its own place, and in itself/Can make a heaven of Hell, a hell of Heaven.'

Náměstí Míru: Large square in Prague.
John Milton, *Paradise Lost*, 2011, Collins Classics.

Brown Bread
Christmas 2006

Christmas had become particularly stressful since John developed dementia and Mum died. This year would be different. I decided to spend the day at home with John, the second time in thirty years.

I walk to his flat. Across Cove Road, down Malwood towards Wickes, past ASDA and PC World, in front of the library, through the underpass, alongside the Technical College and up into Sycamore Road. It takes me half an hour.

Farnborough is silent, seasonally hushed. Few people about: a biker with holly on his helmet purposefully pushing green bottles into the bottle bank; a mother and daughter, who carol Happy Christmas as they swing by, hand-in-hand; a single woman with a laden shopping trolley. And me, alone with the tap of blue safari boots on dry pavement, the scurrying of leaves and litter in the wind. A translucent calm.

We walk back to the house.

'Did I live here with you before?' John asks as I open the door.

'Before' is to be the theme of the day. Before comes and goes, like voile blowing in the breeze of dementia. But today the breeze is delicate, Christmas-soft.

We have coffee, sit and chat. John is tired from the walk.

'I thought we could open our presents later. Will you help me with lunch?'

'Sure.' He jumps up from the chair, eager, content.

'Can you sort out the smoked salmon?'

'What do I have to do?'

I cut open the defrosted pack. 'There's lots for each of us. Not one measly slice each at Christmas.' I am conscious of talking as if he is a child. He giggles. With a knife, I show him how to lift one slice from another.

'Now lay them out on the white plates – overlapping like this. With a slice of lemon.'

'And the end?'

'No, we'll use that for something else. Cut a nice thin slice.'

He points the triangular nose of the knife half way along the lemon. Zest pierces the air.

'No! Not half of it! Here.' He's grinning as I prod the blade sideways with my finger. The breeze returns, wispy and frail.

'Did we get divorced?'

'No, we're still married.'

'Why aren't you wearing a wedding ring then?' I'd taken it off last month.

'Well, we are still married but we don't live together. So it's not quite the same.' I prevaricate.

'Why don't we live together?'

'Because we weren't getting on. Now let's do the bread.'

I take low fat spread from the fridge. The slices of bread are already on a plate. 'Here, spread them thinly, like this.' He copies me carefully. 'Now cut them up.'

'Like this?'

'Triangles are nicer, from corner to corner.' He cuts one while I check the oven.

'Oh look. I've done it wrong.' The second slice is cut into four squares, like building blocks.

'Never mind, Let's see what we can do.' We examine the mismatched slices together.

'How about you cut the triangles in halves, then the squares too? So we have tiny triangles.'

'Won't they look funny?'

'No, they'll be bite-sized.' This time I watch where he places the knife. Bite-sized triangles. 'Perfect.'

Concern cools the kitchen. 'Why didn't we get on?'

'We just didn't. Perhaps we didn't give each other enough space.'

'Really?' He frowns, seeking an answer in the wholemeal.

'Well it must have been my fault. You are so kind to me.' My eyes prick. Memories waft across the kitchen.

'It was both of our faults. We had a bad time. Everything is fine now though. Don't worry.' I sound like my father.

'I just can't remember a thing about all that. I must have blanked it out.'

'Maybe. Perhaps it's for the best. Aren't you happy?'

'Yes. I like spending time with you. I like your house. But I like my flat too.'

'And your own space?' I suggest.

'Mm. Now I'll just sort this lot out.' He's muttering 'my own space' to himself as he arranges the bread.

It's a work of art. Nothing resembling overlapping triangles or parallel lines. John builds our display like an engineer. First, he covers the plate, randomly, with triangles of bread. Then he fills the gaps with the rest. When it's finished the plate is covered by what appears to be one extremely large slice. The display takes on a strange identity. A plate of brown bread, lovingly familiar, but with a twist.

'Pretty,' I breathe, soft as a saudade.

Slipstream

Always behind the pack
bobbing along in their slipstream
the girl with a book on her nose.

I started late, a year after the rest
had given up hope, didn't even realise
Mum chased me to the bus stop
wielding a bundle of bunnies
and a rose-encrusted gizmo.
That day I waddled around
with a rabbit in my knickers
and soggy parts, not a good feeling.
Good for mum though
Jane tipped up with
a red patch on her gymslip
Miss Steadman was kind.
Les anglais sont bien arrivés
bloody foreigners.

Same again forty years later
too busy wading through meltdown
'Do you think it's the menopause?'
asked a friend. 'God knows,
I've never had one before.'
Desert skin, sauna flushes,
monster moods: convenient
labels for chaos, easier
than taming turmoil.
I asked Mum what happened to her
'My periods just stopped,' she said,
a bit like our conversation.

Funny how I missed tampons
and the rhythm of those years
when pain shaped months
and blood meant freedom;

later, I realised this was when
I set up my own business
started writing creatively
became semi-detached
and went travelling, alone –
when the periods just stopped.

Respite

Costa Rica

Off Europe, she lives a life
of duty and teeth-grinding content
in a middle England place where
they colour her primrose pale
paint her widow, forget-me-not
a pallid, closed world.

Off this Pacific Rim of Fire
in a land of rainforest and volcano,
she wanders, unshackled
flits from hibiscus to heliconia
from quetzal to Caribbean
greedy for this gaudy land.

She can't escape the cool winds
the duvet weight of home forever –
for now she scuffs along the sand
plays chicken with the surf.

Sloth

Costa Rica

A gymnast in slow motion,
the three-toed sloth gentles
around a tree-fern, its head
circling as it weaves through leaves
crawls from branch to branch
easy as plants growing.

Slow, slow, soft and slow.

Reptile head, black baby eyes
you creep a four minute metre
edge through an inverted life
clinging by yellow sickle claws
test, touch, avoid, feel
blindingly solitary.

Slow, slow, soft and slow.

Beside a dark, steaming road
I meet a deadly sin
zealous in its perfect balance
here sloth just is
and I too, slow to stop,
do nothing, sloth with you.

Cloud Forest
Costa Rica

When this waiting time is over
I'll travel north from San Jose
along potholed roads and rutted tracks
past hovels, oxen, weathered Ticos
to Poas and the waterfall at La Paz:
where colour calls and hummingbirds
forage off moon-fat insects
and butterflies – a blue morphe
wide as a fist, a zebra longwing
grey, ghostly – graze my arm.

And everywhere warmth falling,
gentle as the rhythm of rain
in that gauzy cloud forest –
soft, misty, still.

Tico: Nickname for Costa Rican.

Hummingbird

A Violet Sabrewing –
rapier deep in the trumpet
of a white hibiscus flower –
curls her claws in ecstasy:
a fluttering, buzzing blur
of lime, aqua, cerise,
suspended in still, moist air.

Time breaks: she retreats,
reels like a drunken sprite,
wipes her bill on a furl of lichen
and glitters away.

Swansong

John didn't want to go out.

'Let's just sit here,' he suggested.

He looked so frail, so old, his fine, thick hair now white and thinning, that increasingly familiar, slightly glazed look in his eyes. As if a light was dimming. He was fading, becoming shadow, shade. My heart clenched with fresh anxiety. John must have sensed it; he took me in his arms, held me close. I could feel the trembling that now often racked his once solid frame.

'I love you,' I said.

'I know you do,' he replied.

'How do you know?' I teased. 'How do you know I don't come to see you because I feel I ought.' He looked at me, assessing. The button-bright Butler boy was back.

'You wouldn't. I know you, Annie. You don't do things because you ought to. Not any more anyway.'

We talked about Jeanne. Then quite suddenly, out of the blue, I burst into tears. It was like projectile vomiting. Suddenly everything coalesced into a Gordian knot of pain. And how I cried. I cried like a baby, cried for our rose-coloured past, the compromised present, the awful future. I cried for John; I cried for me. I cried for everyone who suffers from, or because of, dementia.

'Oh dear me,' he said. 'Come here, little one. Why are you crying? Are you crying because you're alone?' He took me in his arms, murmured 'Don't cry little one. I'll look after you.' Murmured with the cruelty of compassion.

Grief. Such awful grief. Physical pain, as if I were having a heart attack.

Two weeks later John died from an abdominal aortic aneurysm.

Alone

Yesterday I collected your ashes

Strange, they're so heavy
I'd imagined feather-light dust
but even the bathroom scales
register nothing – nothing –

which feels strange so I hop on,
hugging you in my arms,
calculating our new difference:
one stone, one pound.

You're sealed inside the urn,
a deep red poly-carbon pot
tall with squared shoulders
shaped reassuringly like a sweet jar

but on the top an official label
John Sherry, 77 years
Aldershot
cremation number 91608.

Still I'm comforted
by the lifeblood colour of our pot
and its dependable bulk –
solidly present in your absence.

Book of Remembrance x 2

They've reproduced my words precisely

To live on
in the hearts and minds
of those who loved you
is not to die.

I was panting for a mistake, an error
a wayward inkblot, anything
to justify anger instead of tears
but even the letters are precise –
square-cut with chiselled faces
and tight calligraphy smiles
a snake-yellow S
three sculpted capitals, J A C.

I wanted rage instead of this hand
that takes mine
eases me into a chair
magics water from the chapel
and waits.

No need to yell, no mistake.

~

I blunder into the gardens
among old English roses
perfuming the air with referred pain –
Absent Friends, Golden Memories
Blythe Spirit, Grace, Peace.

Behind me, two widows
crinkle cellophane to the sounds of 'My Way'
and you, alone on creamy velum
with a fellow called Knight, who died

two years before your cremation.

An hour later they've shut the book.
I fret all the way home
fumbling for Knight's first name;
I'd like to know who keeps company
with you – on that empty page.

Singing in the Rain

Singing in the Rain became our song
in Folkestone where we bought cagoules
to shelter candyfloss and toffee apple
then hollered in weather-worn unison
all the way home.

Another time, we sploshed back
from your cousins', under a giant umbrella
drunkenly aping Gene Kelly
playing love's fool
together

and at B & Q, before they bounced you out
for interfering with the merchandise
(an umbrella-shaped curtain pole)
on a soggy French Alp, in a rainforest
all throughout this sodden life.

It's nine months now; more rain
hard slaps against the decking
the DVD clouds over as I dance alone
twirling, swirling, prancing
on a carpet puddled with tears.

'Be still' said the Daffodil
Madingley Hall

She's pacing the gardens again
clop, clop, twitch, clop
short-term blocked like the drains
clop, clop, twitch, clop
no fritillaries today, just rain, rain
clop, clop, twitch, clop.

Why can't she stand still
even doze a while? – like me
rolled up in this deep, dark duvet
a happy introvert hunkered down
since the first frosts –
though I'm pleased to see
two worms slither by
shifting and sifting loam
to ready my spring bed.

She'd be better hibernating
instead of trying to force a flower
clop, clop, twitch, clop –
why not give stillness a chance?

Anniversary

St Swithuns, Headbourne Worthy

All year long I've thought this
a good place to scatter your ashes
I'll have to decide one year
but today I just try it out for feel
the perfect place to reflect
on your death, your life – with you.

So we sit together
on this weather-warm bench, among
the lichened gravestones and daffodils
and the Hyde bourne holds us close
in a circle of bright memory
as two swans slide by, silent.

Then, the male rears up,
snorts like a horse, splatters me wet –
back into my here, my now.

Headbourne Worthy: One of the Worthy churches on the banks of the
River Itchen, originally intended for pilgrims approaching the shrine of
St Swithun at Winchester Cathedral.

After Montale
Cinque Terre, Italy

Riomaggiore, Manarola,
Vernazza, Corniglia,
Monterosso al Mare –
villages nested on blue
pecking out a living
in stark sunlight.

Montale guides me
through this sun-baked land
where mosquitoes cloud the air
vines hang from the sky
and the black sea
hollers and howls.

Others worry my mind
with squeaks and squawks,
block views with hunched packs
and clutter that reeks of home,
crushing cuttlefish bones.

And so I climb
clamber and scramble
up towards falcons and kestrels:
here, a scent of *limoni,*
the soft swish of a seagull's wings
and silence –
where only the light sings and rings.

Eugenio Montale, *Cuttlefish Bones*, 1998, Farrrar, Straus and Giroux.

Cargo Class

Such a laugh you had
a force ten gale of a laugh:
you'd rumble at my jokes
(which were never *that* funny)
or boom along with Parky
while upstairs the cat purred
and I tried to read –
dancing words, laughing lines.

You'd laugh at me now:
two-legged cargo
in hard hat and high vis
freighted from Humber to Holland
up Skaggerak, down Kattegat
scuttling from bunk to bridge
skittering from galley to gangway –
a contained hagfish.

You'd feel at home here
in this drumming diesel world
where Germans, Russians and Poles
chew on tonnage and tides
and pilots argue draft, depth, beam;
you'd yarn with the Chief
talk cranes, containers, capacity –
without you I float, drift.

Today, on watch with the kittiwakes:
Captain Kalinin grabs weather
from the Navtex, cracking silence –
Tyne, Dogger, German Bight
good visibility, risk of storms.
'So, we might see thunder,' I bleat.

'Ochen chorosho Anna!
Briteesh joke!' he bellows.
You here after all
in this sailor's happy howl.

Hanging On

For Reverend John Layzell

The caretaker unlocks the chapel
as I trudge across the car park

inside,
so quiet I can hear the air breathe.

I took my seat at the front
between my brother and his wife,
he held my hand like a child.
'Never let go of his hand,' Mum would say
that day, he gripped mine.
A cousin came late, a friend lost his way
someone mumbled through the elegy
but most of us just sniffed, or cried gently.

The pulpit was so close
that I almost reached out, touched it;
instead I stared at you
hung on to your words –
most of which I'd written –
clung to your presence
your faith, wishing it mine,
stared at that sun gold coffin.

Two years on
still hanging on.

Excursion into Colour

Enrolled on this course,
I anticipated romance, rainbows,
chameleons, quetzals,
maybe pigments and paints,
certainly an aurora borealis,
and a few dancing daffodils
to recollect in tranquillity.

Dr Brown's agenda, however,
covered wavelength, frequency,
amplitude, nanoseconds,
Young Maxwell's triangle,
prisms, diffraction, energy,
black bodies, electrons,
and *even* excitable atoms.

After negotiation, we did examine
incandescence, fluorescence,
spectral radiance,
fog bows, moon bows
Parhelia, the Brocken spectre.
And dyer's chamomile, miller blue,
woad, saffron, indigo.

And finally – together – we unearthed
a yomping yellow sapphire.

Tumbling Leaves
Studio, Elgar country

Tumbling leaves on deco Doulton
taupe and dove grey on cream.
'They were my mother's,' she says.

Outside, a patch-welded giraffe
scrumps from a fine, old tree.
Their shadows synchronise.

And the violin's *saudade* –
in the whiffled leaves
in that clef of Malvern Hills
in this scumbled night –
dark light.

A Kind of Vanishing

The path changes texture, becomes a single-track railway line, pitted with rusted sleepers, becomes shingle. Purple bittersweet, red campion, biting stonecrop tucked among the multi-coloured stones. Not a barren beach after all, but cantankerous, protected by sharp prickles and hairy spikes. Gulls scatter as I crunch over the *fulls* and *lows*, terns potter among the ridges. A flash of sky – a common blue on a bristle of oxtongue. Then a tumble of buildings, Tide Mills, once a thriving community, in decline from the 1840s, its past shaped by the tides – and man. Pressured by the repeal of the corn laws and the development of steam-powered roller mills, steam ships. Pressured by the coming of railway and cross-channel ferry services to neighbouring Newhaven. Pressured by developers building over the entrance to the mill creek. But nature wielded the greatest pressure of all. Two massive storms in the winter of 1875/76 filled the millponds with tons of shingle, terminally affecting the mill's capacity. I hunker down with a garlic snail beside the mill race sluice. More shingle here. Everywhere the sounds of insects, toiling, shifting. And the smell of grain, the rackety rack of the wheels grinding flour, the laughter of girls. A lone figure on the sea-shore – the last mill-worker lived here in 1881 – loss gouged into his face. For a time the mill cottages were used by the railway, then the Chaillet Marine Heritage Hospital was built nearby. More pressure. From the matron – the villagers were tipping their sewage into the sea. Finally, from the council, with a Health Order. Cries in the wind now, the screams of women being evicted, the coughs of children in iron bedsteads on the beach. And in the distance, deeper sounds, men swearing as they heave a seaplane from the hangar erected in the ruins during the First World War; explosions as the military demolish Tide Mills in the Second. Sun-bleached sepia worlds. All pressure eased. And long-shore drift sculpting the shingle.

Mooching in Maine

'Hiya Mooch! How'ya doin' today?'

I'm walking along the waterfront towards the Ocean Gate Terminal. Mr Norris is beaming up at me.

Susan had introduced us two days before at the meet-the-author lunch. The same Susan who'd pinned me to the wall with the force of her smile, then subjected me to a double dose of twenty questions, including my reason for being in Portland, Maine.

'I've been staying with friends; now I'm just mooching around.'

Her smile fell.

'Haven't you a hotel?'

'Why, yes I do. I'm staying on Congress Street.'

As she breathed a sigh of relief, I squeezed in a question.

'Why'd you think I've no hotel?'

'Well, here the word *mooch* means to *mooch off* someone as if you're homeless. Americans are touchy about the homeless. Makes them feel guilty. I bet you don't have many homeless. The English are so practical.'

She peers at me, knowingly.

'They have a great sense of humour too, but not when they're in the US.'

I could feel myself losing mine. An older gent in a wheelchair attempted to pass by. His left arm was withered, the hand in a bright red mitten.

'Mr Norris, this lady's from the UK.'

He blinked up. 'Where they call underpasses subways and the metro the toob.'

'She's here on vacation. Says she's mooching around. I told her we don't like that word.'

'Hiya, Mooch,' he winked.

During the author talk I could see him, nodding, agreeing, totally engaged.

And now here he is again, wearing a blue mitten and an even brighter smile.

'I've been looking at that cruiser, something wrong with the side thrusters,' I say.

'Happens quite often, a good enough place to get stranded,' he replies.

I ask if he's from Maine.

'Well, gal, it's a looooong story,' he says, his voice round and rich. 'I'm an architect. Had it all – New York, penthouse apartment, career, girl. Then – a stroke at thirty-nine. Tough call, eh? Came here to convalesce, liked it, stayed. You never know what's round the corner.'

'Exactly,' I say, thinking of the aneurysm that felled my husband.

'Best to go with that there flow, take each day for what it is.'

He wears his disability easily like a soft winter coat. A man happy with his lot.

'I love yer accent, gal. Could listen to you for hours. What d'ya do? Lecture, law?'

'Consult, write a bit.'

'You could be as dumb as a wharf rat and we'd still think you were an Ivy League professor. And your name's Mooch.'

We grin at one another.

'It's what I do.'

'With great skill and enjoyment.' His laugh is low, down in the bass. 'Well it sure suits you, gal. Look me up if you come back.'

He waves his un-gloved hand, swings the wheelchair round in a tight circle, then zooms along the front, doing wheelies and whistling, 'Oh what a beautiful morning.'

Bel Canto

Portland, Maine

A rich stave of colour
        sweeps through the market square
brushing cadenzas and trills
        towards a drab, grey sky.

Over there,
a mixed salad bright with nasturtiums,
mini jacks with eyes, noses, smiles,
pale pink radishes, the size of satsumas,
Maine cider, thick, beige, gloopy,
chromatic carrots – cream, white, yellow –
orange cauliflowers
and a cerise eggplant.

And here,
multi-coloured gourds, squash
with outlandish names, textures to match:
Hokkaido, Spaghetti, frilly Long Pie,
Rouge vif d'Entempes, Buttercup,
Butternut, Sunshine,
Acorn Golden Nugget
and dainty Delicata.

Such sumptuous sounds, classic coloratura,
        like sunlight and sunburst –
or gypsy summer
        in that square of brilliant afternoon.

Counterpoint

We lean on blistered clapboard
squint into a soft, sun-shot haze
try to ignore the camera crew
the itch against our backs.

To our left, fishermen in orange oil-skins
lump lobsters from boat to crate,
crates which young women heave
into the pound, for the off season;
a quiet rush, any later
the lobster can't acclimatise.

Vinalhaven Island: boat-shacks, pickups
hard-bitten homes softened by golden rod
a Galamander in Elder Littlefield blue
the stink of lobster bait.

'Would ya'll mind moving so ya're outa shoot?'
A continuity girl, legs as long as Redwoods,
sidles us behind the ticket booth; he grumbles,
'Life stops when make-believe hits town.'

We sit and wait, listening:
the clapperboard clatters
the gulls bicker
and the ferry arrives.

Grief Goblin

He's a spiteful little bastard, ugly and mean-spirited. No sooner do you think you're doing OK than he comes back and – wham! He pole-axes you back into that black place. This time he came when Janice died, burrowed into my underbelly. Other losses, death especially, always resonate but this one shocked me purple. Though I didn't know her well I'd have liked to. A deep woman, hair like a tropical night.   Serious, often melancholic; later I discovered why. Before she died of non-Hodgkin's lymphoma Janice produced some stunning poetry, spare and rich. We connected and now she too has gone. He's watching as I type, smiling. He's happy that I'm sad. His smile is vicious. It gloats, glooping like over-cooked porridge on a stove. It stinks, smells burnt and old. I am pessimistic when he's around, lacking confidence. Threatened, on the *qui-vive*, tense. As if I'm on a tightrope, about to fall into an infested river. Today I can't get rid of him. Did he come because of Janice? Because I overstretched myself?   Reached too high, like an over-excited child who needs to calm down? As my nanny used to say, 'This will all end in tears.' The grief goblin makes sure it does. And he doesn't listen. He steamrollers fragile self esteem, pushes joy and happiness aside. With him I become a battered wife, relieved one moment, terrorized the next. A creature of shadows, the Grief Goblin lies in wait, brooding. He's jealous, egotistic and ungenerous. He's like a tutor who bullies a sensitive student, tells them they need diminishing because he feels diminished by them. A creature of darkness. I want him out of my life; I fear he will always return.

Colour Break

Peninsula Square, Winchester
planted out with fat yellow tulips,
massed *Triumph,* serried ranks
in parade-ground precision;
among the stiff primary colours
a flare of carmine erupts
like prickly heat – blood on the boil,
one bloom refusing to conform.

A Hmong village
high in the Thamjam mountains,
a shock of strawberry blonde
among the dark Lao Soung;
above sun-fried Nordic cheeks
ice-blue eyes burn into mine
with her absolute need to sell –

a child's imperative to conform.

Winter Sale

A cerise pink fedora perches
on top of a mustard velvet cloche
and tips me a come-closer wink
as I stare into a cave of colour, texture
and shape – *hats* with wondrous names.

A Harriet Bobbie Cap, red French Beret
Panama Bowler, fur felt Bromley
Imogen Tweed, Indiana, Hunter
St Louis Flying Cap, Connoisseur Top Hat
Stingy Brim, Gatsby, a lime Slouch.

Snooks the Hatter ushers me in.
'I was admiring the fedora in the window,
I'm only looking.' His eyebrow knows
a no-go hat – too vivid, too girly, too much.
'Maybe a trilby?'

Now *this* one zings: a deep crown
dimpled above the right eye,
and a tilted brim, quetzal-bright,
mint-fresh, soft as sage
with hints of jade, peacock, emerald.

In *this* hat I can hear Spring.

Wind-Flower

It's Open Day and
he's demonstrating distillation
using a miniature Hagia Sophia;
the retort doesn't fit properly
so he seals it with cornflour paste
that bubbles and blisters
in the heat of the still.
'I'm using an *Intermedia,* Old English –
a blend of *Angustofolia* and *Latifolia* –
luscious, oily, great for distilling.
Smell it.'
Like walking into a lavender bag.

Outside, a light summer rain
mists blue avenues, where
the lavender bag explodes
over and over again
soft and wet against our knees.

'No, you can't really use them as pot plants.
Lavender needs air flow, freedom.
They're unhappy inside, waste away.'

And now, just a week later
one of our rarest flowers,
Portland's own sea lavender –
dense clusters of pinkish-blue
on waving, curved sprays –
seeded and settled
on the limestone cliffs at Church Ope.

Limonium recurvum
laughs at the wind.

Philimhor

Packing up your clothes
I came across the tartan rug
you used to keep in the Zephyr.
I never liked the colours –
far too Santorini, too Colman's –
but that Stuart plaid served us well.
Today, as I fold the rough wool,
I remember other strokes
kinder fingers at work
think of our honeymoon.

All those cheery souls
with their *chip butties 'n tea on't pier*
and Sea View, a place of plenty,
soft burgundy feathers of beetroot
growing between standard roses,
that first taste of tripe
and rashers of local bacon, a foot long –
'We don't waste much in Scarborough' –
her face, happy as an egg, sunny-side up.
What was her name?

And us hidden on the moors
spread over the Stuart plaid:
heather, a curious sheep, birdsong,
love to last a lifetime
and a post-coital tickle on my rear.

Widow-time, the living's not easy.
I swaddle myself tight in tartan,
massage the weave, finger to thumb,
find shelter in this
my own philimhor.

Philimhor: Large tartan plaid typically worn by Scottish drovers.

Epilogue

Just off Old Aberdeen's cobbled High Street lies King's College. The Arts Faculty library, an oak-panelled den of learning, squatted at the rear of the quadrangle, under the Crown Tower, between Elphinstone Hall and the fifteenth century chapel. Inside to the right, south transept style, romance in its capital and lower case guises was to be found. Here many of the class of '71 found both.

My home for four years, this was also home to a tome on Emma Bovary's plate. I remember being amazed that someone could write a whole book about a simple dinner plate. Professor Chalmers was similarly impressed.

'Here is Flaubert at his finest,' he waxed. 'Here realism and emotional subjectivity combine,' he waned.

Toute l'amertune de l'existence lui semblait servie sur son assiette. 'All the bitterness of life seemed to be served to her on her plate.'

A bit like being force-fed Anglo Norman poetry I thought, loathing the lais of Marie de France, while pitying Emma, prisoner of her emotions and the object world.

Yet objects can also affirm; objects, like poetry, can free the fettered mind.

In my home is one such, a kaleidoscope, bought in New York. It is, in fact, a telescope, created by Van Cort, instrument-makers of Maine. An original Charles Bush reproduction, limited edition, number 2499. Handmade. Sleek. A sloping barrel, stocky. Perfect proportions. Ten and a half inches high, nine inches long. Black matt leather, sweet-smelling. One end is encased in a wide brass ring with a miniature ship's wheel. Nudge the wheel and bright splinters float round in oil. Each movement produces an expensive tick-tock of sound. A turned pillar supports the barrel and splays out into four legs, curved like brackets. The light oak, French polished, is honeyed with a brass-like sheen.

Light and colour and movement; the telescope-kaleidoscope also represents precision and quality. And ambiguity. I think of Nelson, Scott, Columbus, headlands, harbours, storms, moonlight on water. Of the *faro di Genova,* the Lanterna. I think about

111

journey, that means of freeing and finding myself, which never leaves me.

I look down the barrel, see the glow of a mandala, benign and beckoning.

Marie de France Lais: Series of twelve short narrative poems, probably composed in the late 12th century, which glorify the concept of courtly love through the adventures of their main characters.